ABCs Naturally

A CHILD'S GUIDE TO THE ALPHABET THROUGH NATURE

Lynne Smith Diebel and Jann Faust Kalscheur
photographs by Jann Faust Kalscheur

Library of Congress Control Number: 2003105889
ISBN: 1-931599-27-0

Cover Photos: Jann Faust Kalscheur

Reprinted
2013
Wild Alphabet Press
316 Grant Street
Stoughton, Wisconsin 53589
wildalphabet.com

To my family. LSD

*To my parents, Keith and Jane,
for nurturing my deep love of nature. JFK*

ACKNOWLEDGEMENTS

Thanks go especially to our families, whose support made this book possible: Gary Kalscheur, Ben Kalscheur, Matt Kalscheur, Bob Diebel, Matt Diebel, Greg Diebel, James Diebel, Anne Diebel, and Rebecca Gass. Thanks to our editor, Stan Stoga, for his support and guidance. Thanks also to Theresa Ganshert, whose artistic guidance shaped the design of the book. And more thanks to the following people for their valuable contributions: Jenny Carroll, Jacky Graves, Jena Sinclair, Sue Reindollar, Kris Kalscheur, Shelley Anderson, Kirsten van der Sterren, Bill Tans, David L. Sperling, Mike Smith, W. Carl Taylor, Wayne Pauly, Mike Maddox, David Sample, Craig Anderson, the Wisconsin DNR's Endangered Resource and Forestry Departments, Jane Carroll, Abraham Ganshert, Rebecca Mackie, Amanda Nelson, Dennis Rupnow, David Bouche, Judy Albertini, Kathy Dutilly, Jim Keeney, Jennifer Fuschino, Doug MacKenzie, Neely Droessler, Christine Droessler, Fran Visek, and Julie Breunig.

In the dark and leafy forest
Yellow birch roots like to play,
Peeking from their mossy hideout,
Calling out the letter

A

Do you see the lily pad
Floating quietly?
It doubles as a boat for bugs
And a bright green letter

B

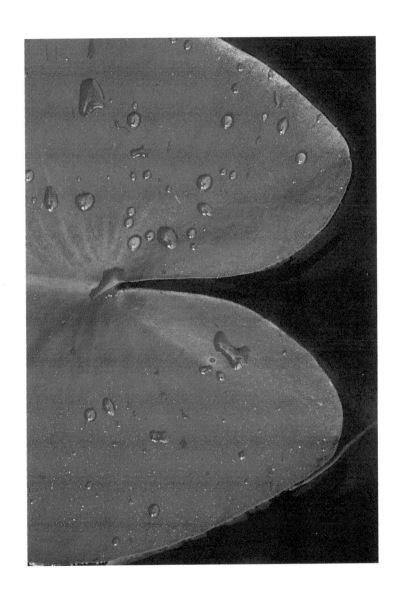

What would you eat for breakfast
If you were a chickadee?
Try frosted foxtail grass seeds
Curled in a tasty

C

A thick old grape vine
Loops around a tree.
Its heavy rope vines curve
Into a snow-covered

D

Little flags of sumac
Flutter softly in the breeze.
Fall has turned the leaves to red
So you can see an

E

Search the forest floor in springtime,
Find what a growing deer has left.
He rubbed his worn old antlers off
And left behind a letter

F

Seeds inside a locust pod
Are cozy as can be,
Tucked away all winter
In their sleeping bag shaped like a

G

On a winter windowpane
Jack Frost's icy fingers trace
Fancy patterns to surprise you,
Like this frosty letter

H

Settlers called it blazing star,
And if you wonder why,
Look closely at its tiny flowers:
Bright stars blaze the letter

I

Flashy-flowered goldenrod
In winter fades away.
Sun-bright blossoms turn to pale,
Curled in a wispy

J

Look in a marshy mirror
On a quiet day
To see if bulrush stems
Reflect the letter

K

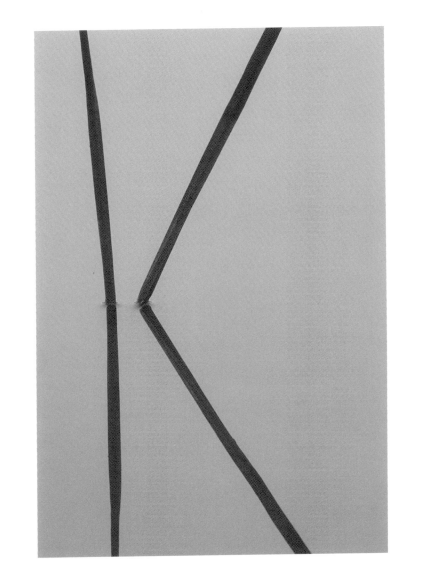

If you brush against a spruce,
It shares a spicy smell.
Wet snow snuggles between its needles,
Helping you see the letter

L.

Cattails grow in mucky marshes;
Long leaves rise up from their stems.
They look like bent and broken swords
And make a leafy letter

M

Walk in a cornfield after the harvest.
The corn is gone and stored in a bin.
Broken stalks are left behind,
Bent into a jagged

N

Have you ever found a songbird nest
That's fallen to the snow?
Its tiny builders may be gone
But they left you a twiggy

If you find a fern in springtime,
This is what you'll see:
A tender little baby plant
Curled up in a

P

Wait for fall to come around
When viburnum berries are in view.
Look for a thick red cluster
With one green leaf to complete the

Q

Summer leaves are soft and tender,
Blurry green seen from afar,
Brown and crisp when autumn comes,
Curled on their stem in a brittle

R

If you visit a flamingo at the zoo,
His bright pink feathers are hard to miss.
His loopy neck may surprise you too
By suddenly curving into an

S

Nestled into dry oak leaves
Underneath a tree,
You may find a fallen branch
That looks just like a

T

Hiding under leaves all summer,
Bittersweet berries stay green and new.
When autumn comes they turn to orange,
Bright berries burst out in a

U

When you go out for a hike,
Rocky shapes are fun to see.
Volcanic basalt worn by weather
Looks just like the letter

V

A turkey walked on slushy ice,
As turkeys sometimes like to do.
And where he walked that winter day
He left a three-toed

W

Is it a bird? Is it a plane?
Is it a cloud playing tricks?
Cirrus cloud and jet trail
Crisscross in an

X

When it was a growing tree
This white birch reached up for the sky.
Now it rots on a bed of leaves,
Looking like a ruffly

Y

Zigging and zagging across the gravel
(And sometimes up the trunk of a tree),
Virginia creeper's crawling vines and
Red fall leaves show you a

Z

FACTS AND FOLKLORE

A *is the surface roots of a yellow birch tree*

Did you know that trees have as many roots hiding underground as they have branches growing up above? The next time you look at a tree, imagine it turned upside down with its branches underground.

A few roots often show themselves on top of the ground. Sometimes these roots even grow right into each other. Look at the picture of the letter A. That's just what those yellow birch roots did.

Many birches have white bark, but the yellow birch's bark is soft, silvery yellow. White birches love to grow in bright sunshine, but yellow birches often grow in the shade of maple forests. Their fluttery little leaves turn yellow in the fall and light up the woods. If you see a yellow birch in springtime, look for its long, fuzzy, hanging catkins. Catkins are the birch's flowers.

Native Americans used bendable young birch trees as poles for their wigwams. They also boiled birch bark for medicines. Many people today like to make furniture and musical instruments from the beautiful, strong wood of this tree.

But forest animals have a different idea. They like to eat this tasty tree. Beavers and porcupines chew up the bark of its roots and trunk. Birds called sapsuckers drink its sweet sap. Squirrels and birds gobble up its catkins and seeds. Snowshoe rabbits nibble the leaves and twigs of baby birches. Moose and white-tailed deer get a good meal from the tender little branches and leaves of taller trees. The yellow birch is like a forest grocery store for animals.

B *is the leaf, or lily pad, of a yellow pond lily.*

If you were a moose, you might like to stand in shallow water and munch on the pond lily's tasty seedpods. People sometimes like to eat pond lilies too. Native Americans and early settlers used to go out in canoes to gather pond lilies. They roasted the seeds and ate them like popcorn. They ground the roasted seeds into meal to make bread or mush. They dried and ground the roots to make medicines.

If you were a bug or a frog, you might use a lily pad as a rest stop or a launch pad. An author named Beatrix Potter wrote a story about a frog called Jeremy Fisher who used a lily pad as his fishing boat.

Lily pads float on the surface of quiet water. They look like little boats, but they can't move as much as boats can. They are anchored by strong stalks rooted in the mud at the bottom of the lake. The beautiful, yellow pond lily flower grows on its own stalk. When the flower is done blooming in midsummer, it becomes a fat pod filled with seeds.

When you visit a pond, a stream, or a marsh, look for pond lilies in places where the water is usually quiet. If the wind is blowing, the edges of the lily pads will turn up on the side that the wind is blowing from. You will see that the shiny green lily pad has a purple underside.

C *is a bristly foxtail grass seed head, frosted with snow.*

Can you guess how foxtail grass got its name? Its seed head is covered with soft, furry bristles like a real fox's tail. The seed head even curves like a fox's tail. To have a little fun with foxtail grass, squeeze a seed head through your hand. It will move like a wooly-bear caterpillar.

You won't have any trouble finding this grass. Foxtail grasses first grew in Africa. They traveled to Europe and then to the United States as hitchhikers in people's luggage. Now these grasses grow all over our country. In the fall, look for a tall grass stem with a fuzzy seed head that curves into a C shape.

Most people in America think of foxtail grass as a weed, because it grows where they don't want it to grow. But many birds love to eat foxtail grass seeds. For a better look at those delicious little seeds, use a magnifying glass. The seeds are hiding under the bristles.

Your favorite breakfast cereal is made from grass seeds. Rice, oats, corn, wheat, barley, and rye—the cereal plants—are all cousins of the grasses that birds eat. So now, when you eat your cereal in the morning, you can tell everybody that you are "eating like a bird."

D *is the vine of a wild frost grape.*

Long ago, when Vikings first sailed to America, they saw so many wild grapevines growing here that they called this country Vinland—"the land of wild grapes." Wild frost grapes are a true American plant.

Frost grapes got their name because their sour little purple grapes turn sweet after the first frost. That's when people like to pick wild frost grapes to make grape jelly, grape juice, or wine.

The vines of the frost grape can grow up to 45 feet long and several inches thick. If a thick vine is hanging from a big tree, it may even be strong enough to swing on.

Grapevines love to wrap around big trees. A young growing vine uses its tendrils like little fingers to hold on to the tree. A frost grapevine can live over a hundred years. An oak tree also lives a long time. A grapevine and an oak could grow old together, like good friends.

E *is smooth sumac leaflets in their red fall clothes.*

Once there was a man who didn't like sumac. He built his house in a field where sheep had once grazed. The sheep had eaten up almost everything in the field. All the baby trees and bushes were gone. The only thing left was grass. When the sheep left, the man hoped that the beautiful grass would keep growing around his house. But sumac bushes grew instead!

Every summer he cut the sumac down. He hauled away great piles of sumac branches. But the smooth sumac just kept coming back. It popped up everywhere.

The man didn't know that when you cut down sumac, it grows even faster and stronger. Sumac spreads by sending out roots underground to grow new plants. Years ago, when prairie fires burned large areas of land, the sumac was killed and other plants took its place. Now firefighters put out prairie fires before they can do their sumac removal work, because fires are dangerous to people and their homes.

In the days when sumac wasn't such a problem for people, Native Americans used smooth sumac to make things. They boiled the bark, roots, and berries for medicines and teas. They also used the roots, bark, leaves, and berries to make beautiful colors of dye—orange, yellow, red, and brown.

If the man had known all these things, he could have had fun with his smooth sumac instead of being mad at it.

F *is a white-tailed deer antler,*
nestled in reindeer moss that looks like tiny antlers.

Native American legend tells how the deer got its antlers. Long ago, the deer and the rabbit were bragging about how fast they could run. They decided to have a race to see which was faster. As a prize, the other animals would give the winner a crown. On the morning of the race, the rabbit was caught chewing a path through the bushes so it could take a shortcut. The other animals called the rabbit a cheater and gave the crown of antlers to the deer.

This crown belongs to the male deer, or buck. He uses his set of antlers (also called a rack) to fight other bucks, and he marks his territory by rubbing his rack on trees. A buck sheds his antlers every winter and grows new ones every spring. Each of his two main antlers has branches, which are called points because they point upward.

Some people say that a really old buck will have the most points. Scientists say that the best way to tell a deer's age is to be a deer dentist and check the deer's teeth. Unless you are a scientist, don't try this!

Native Americans say that if you find antlers in the woods, you won't grow old. Antlers that have been shed don't grow old either. Hungry mice and squirrels love to gnaw away the antlers for the calcium in them.

If you want to try to find the antlers of a white-tailed deer, don't wait until summer. They may be all eaten up. Look for them between January and April. Hike in areas where you know that deer live. If you can find a deer path, follow it. Look on the ground on both sides of the path. Sometimes a deer will catch its old antlers in bushes and pull them off, so look up in the branches too. Good hunting!

G *is the curled seedpod of the common honey locust tree.*

The first time you see a common honey locust tree, you will probably be surprised. Pointing straight out from its trunk are big thorns. These thorns are often four inches long and have three points. Thorns cover its branches too.

In the fall the honey locust is decorated with long, dangling seedpods. When cattle and deer find these pods, they are very happy. They love to eat the pods because they are filled with sweet, tender seeds and pulp. The sweetness is why the tree is called a "honey" locust. When the pods fall to the ground during the fall and winter, rabbits and quail feast on them too. The honey locust is a cousin to the pea plant, so its seeds are nutritious, just like peas.

Honey locust trees can live a long time. A big old honey locust stands at the Gettysburg Cemetery in Pennsylvania. It was standing near President Abraham Lincoln when he spoke his famous Gettysburg Address in 1863.

H *is lines of lacy hoarfrost.*

On nippy mornings, you may find frosty artwork on your bedroom windows. Legend says that Jack Frost draws on windows (and on lots of other things) with his icy fingers. The tale of Jack Frost comes from an old Norse myth about an icy elf named Jokul ("icicle") Frosti ("frost"). English speakers decided to call him Jack Frost instead, but they still say he makes the frost.

Scientists have a different explanation for frost. If the temperature outside a house is below freezing, the glass of a storm window, or outside window, also becomes that cold. Inside the house, warm, moist air from people's breath sneaks into the cold air between the inside window and the storm window and turns into water vapor. If the storm window is cold enough, this water vapor freezes right on the glass of the storm window into what is called "hoarfrost."

Hoarfrost forms in beautiful patterns for your enjoyment in the morning. These patterns are even more interesting to look at with a magnifying glass. Like snowflakes, no two frost patterns are ever just the same. In the picture of the H, the hoarfrost forms a pattern that looks like lines of snowflakes or frosted barbed wire.

Hoarfrost may also look like feathers or ferns. When "fern frost" forms, that means it is very cold outside. When it's that cold, people are fond of saying that Jack Frost is nipping at their noses.

I *is the flower of the prairie blazing star.*

If you like watching butterflies, try growing prairie blazing star in your yard. Its flowers are magnets for butterflies and bees. Prairie restoration areas in late summer are also a good place to see blazing star. If you are lucky, butterflies may be there too, enjoying the blazing-star flowers' nectar.

Blazing star gets its name from its clusters of bright flowers, which are shaped like many-pointed stars. When blazing star blossoms begin to bloom in late summer, the ones at the top of the stalk open first, instead of opening from the bottom up. Blazing star is the only flower that does this.

Some other prairie plants with interesting names are close cousins of blazing star. Kansas gay feather and button snakeroot have flowers that look almost the same as blazing star flowers.

Blazing star's hot pink starflowers are fun to look at with a magnifying glass. And just imagine how beautiful huge fields of blooming blazing star and its relative, goldenrod, would have looked to settlers travelling across the tallgrass prairie in the fall.

J *is an aging goldenrod flower in winter.*

You probably know what goldenrod looks like when it blooms. Goldenrod gives everyone a big, bright yellow flower show every fall. If you ask people what else they know about goldenrod, many will answer, "It causes hay fever!"

But this is not true because goldenrod gets blamed for something that another plant causes. Goldenrod blooms in the fall at the same time as an ordinary-looking plant called ragweed. Each ragweed releases billions of tiny pollen grains with tiny sharp hooks on them, which are blown by the wind. This sharp-hooked pollen blows into peoples' noses and causes lots of hay fever.

Goldenrod flowers don't cause hay fever because they have fat, sticky pollen grains, which can't be blown by the wind. But since there is so much goldenrod around in the fall, with its bright, show-off flowers, people notice it more than they notice plain green ragweed. They blame goldenrod for all the sneezing trouble that ragweed quietly causes. This is a little bit like the times when you get blamed for something your brother or sister did.

K *is two bulrush stems reflected in still water.*

If you find some bulrushes in a local marsh, you can feel how strong and flexible the stems are. Native Americans used bulrush stems to weave baskets and floor mats and to make thatched roofs for their huts.

Some tribes also discovered that the hollow bulrush stems float very nicely. They made canoe-shaped rafts by tying together long, fat bundles of bulrush stems, which can grow up to ten feet tall. They then tied the bundles together with cords made from cattail leaves. Since cattails and bulrushes often grow together, a canoe builder could gather everything he needed in one place.

Native Americans even made floating duck decoys out of small bundles of bulrush stems. They tied the bulrush bundle into a duck shape and decorated it with feathers and plant dyes. A duck hunter could hide among the bulrushes in the marsh and use the decoy to lure his dinner. The duck hunter would probably be successful because ducks like to live where bulrush grows. Wild ducks eat lots of bulrush seeds for their own dinners.

If the hunter didn't catch a duck for his dinner, he could dig up fat bulrush roots from the shallow water. Young, tender roots were eaten raw. Older ones were boiled and mashed for a tasty meal that is like mashed potatoes.

People still use bulrush for weaving things, but it has an even more important job today. Bulrush plants do a very good job of filtering and cleaning polluted water. They also keep shorelines from eroding. Environmental scientists say that planting bulrushes can help us fix the messes we make of our ponds, lakes, streams, and rivers.

L *is a frosted white spruce branch.*

People like to use white spruce trees as Christmas trees. Birds and squirrels are fond of eating the seeds that grow in spruce cones. When spruce trees are young and tender, pesky porcupines chomp on their tasty bark. Black bears sometimes strip off young spruce bark for the sweet sapwood.

Long ago, Native Americans used tough, flexible white spruce roots to lace together their birch bark canoes. Today, people mostly like to make paper pulp out of spruce trees. Strong, light spruce wood is also sometimes used to make things, like the sounding boards of pianos and violins. A tall spruce tree can be used to make a mast for a sailboat.

A tall white spruce is often chosen to stand in front of the nation's capitol in Washington, D.C., during the Christmas holidays. In 2001, the tree was a 74-foot-tall white spruce. After the holidays, the tree was made into lumber that was used to build Habitat for Humanity homes.

A really big white spruce can be 150 feet tall and over 3 feet in diameter. Some big white spruces are almost 300 years old. In the Black Hills of South Dakota, old white spruce trees are covered with a hairy-looking hanging lichen called "old-man's beard." These spruce trees look like the old men of the hills.

M *is tired-out, old cattail leaves.*

It is easy to spot cattails in a marsh—look for their catkins. These are the brown, fuzzy, sausage-shaped flowers that grow at the top of the tall stalks. In the fall, catkins become a fruit. They turn fluffy white as they release huge numbers of puffy seeds.

A catkin looks a little like a short cat's tail. In England, people also call cattails "reed mace." Long ago, British children thought that the brown catkin-on-a-stalk looked like a medieval club called a mace. Boys liked to play with this toy weapon.

Native Americans and American settlers had other uses for cattails. Cattail leaves were handy for weaving mats and baskets. The fluffy fall seeds of the catkin fruit are soft and absorbent, so they used the fluff to make bandages and diapers.

People used to like to eat the thick roots prepared like potatoes. The roots were also dried and ground to make flour. Tender underwater stems were cooked as a vegetable. Cooked catkin flowers are tasty.

Animals are fond of cattails too. Geese and muskrats eat the roots. Muskrats use the leaves to build their lodges. Blackbirds build their nests in cattail marshes.

Modern people are learning that cattails, just like bulrushes, help clean our polluted water and keep our shorelines from eroding. So, the next time you visit a cattail, tell it thanks for being such a useful plant.

N *is a pair of tattered cornstalks.*

A field of cornstalks standing in interesting poses can be a fun place to visit. Crows and deer like to visit winter cornfields too. They are looking for leftovers from the farmer's harvest.

Native American farmers were raising corn long before European farmers arrived in America. Some tribes still plant what they call "three sisters" gardens—of corn, beans, and squash. Those three plants help each other grow. The sister seeds are planted together in a mound of dirt. The strong cornstalks grow into beanpoles for the bean vines to climb. The beans give corn and squash the nitrogen they need. The squash leaves shade the ground, keeping the water in and the weeds out. And all three sisters feed the people.

Native Americans gave the wonderful gift of their brightly colored corn to the first European colonists, who had never seen corn before. The colonists called it maize. Maize kept the colonists from starving.

Today, it is popular to cut a maze pattern of pathways in fields of tall maize for visitors to explore. A modern "maize maze" can be a fun way for you to visit some growing corn plants.

Corn grows tall very quickly in the hot summer. Some people say they can hear it growing, especially at night. An old saying says that a good crop of corn should be knee-high (that's knee-high to a grownup) by the Fourth of July. If you ask a farmer for a knee-high stalk of his corn to play with, you can find out what's inside. Just slice the stalk down the middle. Be sure to ask a grownup to help you do this. Inside, you will find tiny ears of corn just waiting to push their way out of the stalk as it grows.

O *is an abandoned songbird nest lying on the snow.*

Birds' nests are hard to see in the leafy days of summer. Birds hide them to protect their eggs and their babies, and you should never disturb nesting birds. Once those babies are grown, all the birds (even mom and dad) leave the nest. Look around in the winter. It looks as though the trees and bushes have nests in them that weren't there before. They were there, but you just couldn't see them until the leaves fell.

Sometimes nests fall, too, like the nest in the photograph for O. The songbirds who wove this neat little grassy cup for their eggs left a long time ago. Winter winds blew their tiny summer home out of the low bush where they had built it and down onto the snow. Then along came some little white-footed mice, who decided the nest would make a handy winter food pantry.

In the photograph, you can probably see the round seed pits in the nest cup. If you look closely, you can see holes in these wild black cherry pits. Mice nibbled open the pits to eat cherry seeds for a winter meal.

Sometimes mice will make a cover for an abandoned nest pantry like this. They don't want other creatures to find their seeds, so they pile cattail fluff over the nest. If you hike in areas where white-footed mice and cattails live, watch for a fallen nest with a mound of fluff on it. It will look a little like a short, fat ice cream cone.

P *is the fiddlehead of a northern lady fern.*

This fiddlehead isn't the curly end of a violin. It's a coiled-up young lady fern leaf. When it's all uncoiled, it will be a grownup fern leaf, or frond. Lady ferns love to grow along streams in shady northern forests. You can spot them by looking for delicate, lacy fronds that are tapered at both ends and droop at their tips. You don't need to find lady ferns to see a fiddlehead, though. Most ferns sprout this way.

Ferns have no flowers, so they spread by making spores. If you can find some lady ferns in July or August, use your magnifying glass to look at the undersides of the fronds. You may see lots of little brown bumps shaped like the letter J. These are spore cases. Be careful not to bump the plants, because their smooth stalks break easily.

Lady ferns have fat roots, called rhizomes, that spread underground. When they spread, the fronds often grow in a circle. The center of the circle then gradually dies away and a thick ring of ferns forms.

A big ring of northern lady ferns is a favorite treat for grizzly bears. Grizzlies stuff themselves with lady fern fronds whenever they can. You probably don't want to be looking at lady ferns when grizzly bears are snacking on them.

Q *is berries on a viburnum bush called a wayfaring tree.*

Nothing makes a flock of birds called cedar waxwings happier than the sight of a viburnum bush loaded with juicy, ripe berries. Cedar waxwings love to stuff themselves on viburnum berries. But they are also very polite birds. When they sit next to each other on a branch in a row, one will pick a berry. But instead of eating the berry himself, he will pass it on to his neighbor before picking another one for himself. It is their habit to be polite. But it is also their habit to eat lots of viburnum berries.

Occasionally, viburnum berries that have been on the bush for a while will ferment. That means that their juices turn to alcohol. If waxwings eat the fermented berries, they may get a little intoxicated. But they are still polite.

The viburnum in the picture of Q is called a wayfaring tree (even though it's a bush and not a tree), but there are many kinds of viburnum. Native Americans used the straight young stems of the arrowwood viburnum for the shafts of their arrows. Long ago, stern schoolteachers used the stems of the withe rod viburnum to punish students; fortunately, those days are long gone.

People still like to make jelly from the tart berries of some kinds of viburnum, including the American cranberry bush viburnum. This name makes it sound as though this viburnum is related to the cranberries we eat at Thanksgiving, but it's not. If the berries of an American cranberry bush escape those hungry cedar waxwings, the berries will hang on their bush all winter, bright red against the snow.

R *is dried rosinweed leaves.*

If you were a child long ago, when American prairies bloomed with acres and acres of bright flowers, you would have liked finding some yellow-flowered rosinweed. If you break the stem of a blooming rosinweed plant, a blob of pleasant-smelling resin oozes out. Native Americans and settlers would gather the sticky resin into a little ball and chew it, to clean their teeth and freshen their breath. Rosinweed resin was prairie chewing gum.

Rosinweed is harder to find today, because those big, beautiful prairies have been gobbled up by farms and towns. But if you spot a tall plant with a cluster of bright yellow flowers that look like small sunflowers on its top, you may have found some rosinweed. Touch the stem and the leaves. They should feel rough, like sandpaper. Of course, the best way to tell is to break a stem and see if spicy-smelling resin oozes out. But rosinweed is rare in some areas, so it's better just to look and not to break the stem.

In the late fall, when Jack Frost has done his work, the dried rosinweed leaves and seed head still cling to their stalk, curled into interesting shapes. Like with other prairie plants, the leaves and seed head may stay on the stalk all through the winter.

The rosinweed in the picture for R is called wholeleaf rosinweed because its leaves do not have scallops. A rosinweed plant with deeply scalloped leaves near the ground is also called a compass plant. The scalloped leaves of a compass plant almost always point north and south, so travelers long ago could find their way across the endless prairies by checking a compass plant. Chewing gum and a compass—what a handy plant.

S *is the long neck of an American flamingo.*

Have you ever seen a flamingo yard ornament? Some people like flamingos so much that they decorate their yards with lots of bright pink, plastic flamingo statues. Real flamingos also like to live in big groups, called colonies. Many thousands of flamingos can live in one colony.

When it's time to lay its eggs, the flamingo makes a volcano-shaped mud nest. The nest is about a foot high and holds one big, white egg. The parents take turns sitting on the egg. In a colony, many flamingos nest at the same time during the year. Try to imagine thousands of bright pink birds with long necks all sitting on volcano-shaped mud nests at the same time.

Most of the flamingo chicks in a colony hatch at about the same time. They are born with fluffy white feathers and bright pink bills and legs. They are very social, just like their parents. They trot around the colony in groups when they are only a week old. As they get older, their feathers become bright pink, just like those of their parents.

If you see a flamingo, it will probably be in the zoo. Its feathers may be paler pink than those of a wild flamingo. The bright pink feathers of a wild flamingo come from its favorite food, tiny shellfish. Shellfish contain lots of carotene. Carotene is what makes carrots orange and flamingos bright pink.

T *is a fallen tree branch, lying among red oak leaves and wood anemones.*

The floors of forests are usually very messy. Lots of fallen branches, unraked dead leaves, and even dead trees litter the ground. Even though most people wouldn't want their yards to look like this, this is how nature wants her forests to be.

When strong winds blow through a forest, the trees sway and shake. Dead branches that are still clinging to the trees break off and fall to the ground. If a dead branch breaks off a tree, it doesn't hurt the tree at all. In fact, the tree will grow better with the deadwood gone. The deadwood will rot on the forest floor, quietly turning into dirt.

Of course, turning a branch into dirt takes a while. The first change that happens to a dead branch is that its bark rots and falls off. This is what has happened to the branch in the picture for T. Then the wood itself gets softer and softer and finally crumbles. The minerals that went into growing the branch return to the soil. The energy that went into growing the branch feeds organisms like lichens, fungi, and bacteria. These cleanup creatures feed on rotting wood and dead leaves. They help recycle the wood and leaves into very nutritious dirt. Forest plants, from flowering wood anemones to new trees, like to grow in this good dirt.

The next time you see a fallen branch, check first to see if it makes a letter. If it doesn't, don't just pass it by. Look for interesting lichens and fungi on it. Think about how, the next time you see it, it may have rotted away to feed some fungi.

U *is two tangled clusters of burst-open bittersweet berries.*

Bright bittersweet berries will really catch your eye. The "capsules" that hold the seeds burst open when the first frost touches them. This exposes the darker orange or red seed inside. You can see how the capsules burst open in the U picture. These fancy berries grow on vines that wrap themselves around fences, trees, and shrubs.

The bittersweet in the picture is the American bittersweet, but there are two other kinds of bittersweet vines. They all look similar, but only American bittersweet is a native American plant. Of the two others, one kind came from Europe and the other from Asia. The Asian bittersweet is "invasive." This means that it grows out of control and crowds out native plants. Its strong, fast-growing vine can even choke a small tree and kill it. The European bittersweet has deadly poisonous berries and leaves.

Bittersweet is beautiful to look at, but you probably shouldn't pick it for several reasons. American bittersweet is endangered because so many people have cut it for decorations. European bittersweet is poisonous. And even though it would be fine to pick the invasive Oriental bittersweet, it is so hard to tell the three apart that you might be picking one of the others.

V *is volcanic rock.*

If you like to hike in rugged areas, you may meet some very old rocks. The rock in the picture of V, for example, is over a billion years old.

This dark rock is called basalt. It formed over a billion years ago when volcanic lava flowed onto the earth's surface and then cooled and hardened. After the basalt formed, water and wind wore it down, carving it into different shapes. The V shape in the picture is a section of the basalt that collects water after a rain. Water makes the rough and weathered basalt look darker, so the wet shape of the V stands out.

The steep rock walls that sometimes appear alongside rivers are often a good place to see some of the rocks that make up the earth's surface. In a river valley with steep rock walls, the river has flowed for so many years that it has cut a channel through the rock. If you hike in an area like this, look carefully at the layers of rock that form the walls. They tell the story of how our earth's surface grew and changed.

W *is a wild turkey track in the ice of a shallow creek.*

In the morning after a fresh snow, you will often find tracks in your back-yard. Rabbits, birds, squirrels, cats, and dogs leave their footprints for you to follow. If you have a book on tracks or someone to teach you, you can learn what animal made each track. Tracks are a little story of the animal's journey around your yard. The more you know about the tracks, the better the story is.

Forests are full of tracks and stories too. Animals you don't usually see in your backyard, like wild turkeys, leave their prints in the snow, ice, soft dirt, mud, and sand of the forest. Native Americans who lived in forests often drew or carved pictures of wild turkey tracks onto rocks. They were interested in tracking turkeys because they liked to eat them.

The wild turkey lives where the forest is the thickest. It likes to live near oak trees because it likes to eat acorns. It also likes to sleep in a tree at night. A wild turkey looks a little like a farm turkey, the kind that you often see at Thanksgiving dinner. But farm turkeys can't sit in trees and they can't fly. They just waddle. A wild turkey can fly as fast as a horse can run.

You might be able to find a wild turkey track if you look in areas where you know that turkeys live. Look for three-inch-long toe marks. If you are lucky, you may even find a turkey feather.

X *is a jet contrail crossing a cirrus cloud.*

Sailors used to predict the weather by watching the sky. They would "read" the story that the clouds told them and remember it in funny little rhymes, like this one:

Mares' tails and mackerel scales,
Make tall ships carry low sails.

What are mares' (horses') tails doing up in the sky, you ask? Mares' tails are what sky-watchers call high cirrus clouds. Strong winds, high in the sky, stretch cirrus clouds into long, white, wispy things that look like a mare's tail. Mackerel (fish) scales are the name for lower clouds that the wind spreads out in a fish scale pattern.

In the days of sailing ships with tall masts, a captain knew that mares' tails and mackerel scales meant strong winds and rough weather were coming. The captain of a ship at sea would tell his sailors to lower the sails. Lowering the sails would save the ship's tall masts from being broken by the strong winds.

A jet contrail (condensation trail) is made of white ice crystals, just like a cirrus cloud. When a jet plane first leaves its icy trail, the contrail looks like a wide, white marker line on the blue sky. Then it's easy to tell that it's a contrail, not a cirrus cloud, because you can still see the trail coming out of the jet. If the air is quiet way up there where jets fly, the trail keeps its shape. But if the winds are blowing, the trail gets stretched, just like cirrus clouds. The older a contrail is, the more stretched out and wispy it becomes. You could say that:

Old jet contrails,
Can look like mares' tails.

Y *is a rotting birch trunk decorated with lovely lichens and fancy fungi.*

It's easy to like lichens. You can have fun studying their many interesting shapes and colors. Look closely at the picture for Y. Those bright blue blotches are lichens.

Lichens work with their close friends, the fungi, to turn dead trees into dirt. In fact, a lichen is really a fungus with algae cells growing inside of it. The wonderful thing is that the fungus and the alga grow together, as if they were one thing. They take care of each other. The algae have chlorophyll, so they can make food from sunlight to feed themselves and the fungi. The fungi protect the tiny algae cells and suck food from the dead plants that lichens grow on.

Many fungi are not part of a lichen. Mushrooms and toadstools are fungi. The ruffled-looking fungi growing on the Y are also feeding on the wood of the dead birch. It will probably take about ten years for this lichen-fungi team to chew and digest this birch trunk into dirt.

Lichens are a great clean-up crew for the forest. They also hate polluted air, so scientists like to use lichens as an inexpensive way to tell whether air is polluted.

Z *is a Virginia creeper vine on a gravel railroad bed.*

If you mention Virginia creeper to a person who lives in Virginia, he or she might think you're talking about a train or a hiking trail. For many years, a steam train with the nickname "Virginia Creeper" crept through the mountains of Virginia. The tracks were so steep that passengers could get out and walk faster than the train could move. Lots of Virginia creeper vines also grow along the railway. The train was famous for its wonderful shivery-sounding steam whistle. After the train made its last run, in 1977, its rail bed was made into a trail for hikers, bicyclists, horses, and dogs. It's called the Virginia Creeper Trail.

If you like wild grapevines, you will like the Virginia creeper vine too. It grows even longer than a grapevine and much faster. A stem can grow twenty feet a year. It doesn't just grow on the ground. Long, branching tendrils with sticky pads on their tips help it climb up any tree, shrub, or building it meets. These pads are very sticky. Just one five-branched tendril (like a hand), with its pads stuck to a brick wall, can hold a ten-pound weight.

If you are very patient, you might like to watch a Virginia creeper tendril coil. Find some Virginia creeper that is climbing over a shrub. It climbs by coiling its long tendrils around small branches. If a tendril has just started to coil around a branch, you can actually watch the coiling happen. Get comfortable and watch for about a half-hour. The tendril should loop itself all the way around the branch while you watch.

In the fall, birds like to eat Virginia creeper's blue-black berries. Never eat these berries yourself because they are poisonous to people. You might mistake Virginia creeper for poison ivy because it looks a little like that dangerous vine. But Virginia creeper always has five leaflets in each group, while poison ivy has three. Virginia creeper leaves won't make you itch as much as poison ivy leaves, but touching them can cause a rash in some people. *Leaves of five or three, let it be!*

BECOMING AN ALPHABET HUNTER

The idea for this book began when two little boys found an empty clamshell half-buried in the sand of a Wisconsin River sandbar. The five-year-old, who had just learned the alphabet, excitedly showed his brother and his mother, a nature photographer, that the open shell looked like the letter B, the first letter of his name. Their mother photographed the B and thus began their family alphabet hunt tradition.

You don't need to be a nature photographer to start turning your own walks into alphabet hunts. You just need your sharp eyes, curiosity, and a willingness to look at the world a little differently. Oh yes, it also helps to have a good companion.

If you've ever played the alphabet game (finding letters on road signs) in the car on a long road trip, you know how much fun it can be to find the next letter. When you do finally get to the Z, you always want to start over again. An alphabet hunt can be just as fun, but it takes longer to look for letters in nature's shapes than on road signs.

In very early times, letters started out as picture symbols, some of them of shapes found in nature. For example, the letter A started out as a picture of an ox's head. These picture symbols slowly turned into our modern letters, which stand for sounds instead of things like oxen. But if you turn it upside down, an A still looks a little bit like an ox's head with its nose pointing down and its horns pointing up.

Even when you're not trying to find them, nature's letters will sometimes jump out at you. A grandmother and her granddaughter were walking together, talking. The little girl stopped suddenly and exclaimed, "Grandma, there's a Y in our woods!" She pointed to a tree trunk with its top lopped off. Two branches had sprouted from the trunk, one on each side. The branches reached upward to form the arms of a Y.

Other times, you'll need to be patient and study things a bit to find the next letter. When you're in the mood to look for letters, here are some simple ideas to help you see a little differently.

Look in a broad area.

When you get to an interesting place on your hunt, stop walking and look all around you. Turn very slowly in a full circle. Let your eyes slide over the amazing variety of shapes and patterns that nature offers. Look closely at the big shapes of trees, bushes, rock formations, and clouds. Do this broad sweep several times, pausing if a shape or pattern catches your eye. Then look carefully at the smaller parts of the big shape, like a single blade of grass or a few loops of a grapevine.

When you really look around you, searching for a letter shape, you will see things that you wouldn't notice if you were busy walking and talking with someone. The more you look, the more you will see.

Look from a different angle.

We are all used to seeing nature from a straight-on, standing-up point of view. If you want to see something differently—a tree, for example—try a mouse's-eye view. Lie on your back next to the tree trunk and look up toward the sky. The familiar shapes of branches and twigs will look new and different when you see them from where a mouse sees them.

While you're down there, roll over on your stomach and get a close-up look at the stems, seeds, and flowers of grasses and of other plants that are around you. This could be called a butterfly's-eye view, because a butterfly flutters from flower to flower.

After you've spent some time on the ground getting dirty, try a bird's-eye view. Stand up and move like a bird gliding low over the earth. Look straight down at flowers, grasses, tree roots, and fallen branches. If you happen to be near a pond, stream, or lake that has some water plants by the shore, wade into the shallow water and pretend you're a long-legged water bird, waiting patiently for a fish lunch. Slowly study the shapes of lily pads, bulrushes, cattails, floating sticks, and algae.

It's also fun to drop your head down and look between your legs at any natural object. If you've ever tried looking at the world in this upside-down way, you know that things look very different from the way you see them standing straight up. A letter that wasn't noticeable before may suddenly appear! And if it doesn't, you can still have a good time looking around from your upside-down point of view. Just don't get too dizzy.

A change of season offers a different angle too. The same park you walked in during the lush, green, leafy summer will look different when bright-colored fall leaf shapes begin to stand out. Or when branches are bare and outlined with snow in winter. Or when little spring sprouts start to show. An alphabet can take a long time to collect, so waiting for the seasons to change can be a good way to find a new letter.

Look through a magnifying glass.

If you carry a magnifying glass on your walk, you can look closely at the strands of a spider's web, the inner walls of an abandoned bird's nest, the lichens on a dead tree, or the veins of a leaf. These mini-patterns, especially the spider web, may offer you a letter or two. A spider web covered with morning dew is fascinating to see through a magnifying glass.

At home on icy mornings, use a magnifying glass to look at frost crystals that formed during the night on your windows. A whole new world of shapes opens up when you magnify things. It's kind of like what Alice in Wonderland saw when she went down the rabbit hole. Your backyard will seem brand new when you magnify things in it. Looking through a magnifying glass is also like putting a little picture frame around those interesting shapes—which brings us to our next idea.

Look through a frame.

For a fun way to look at any natural scene, try making a cardboard frame to carry on your walks. Use an 8-by-11-inch piece of lightweight cardboard. It needs to be just heavy enough that it will stay flat when you hold it up. Measure and cut out a 4-by-6-inch window in the center of the cardboard. Hold the frame about six inches from your face and look around. When you look at the world through this window, you focus your attention. You only see what's in the window, so you see it better. You will be surprised at how different the natural world looks when you frame different parts of it.

COLLECTING YOUR OWN ALPHABET

You may be happy just seeing lots of letters in nature. But if you want to collect your own alphabet, there are several ways you can do this. One way is to carry a simple point-and-shoot camera, loaded with outdoor film, on your walks. A child can use a camera like this as easily as an adult can.

A camera frames things for you, just like the cardboard frame described above. If you remember to try lots of the different angles described earlier—mouse's-eye, butterfly's-eye, bird's-eye, upside-down, as well as straight-on—looking through a camera may even help you find your next letter. If you find a letter while looking upside down, go ahead and shoot it right side up. Then just flip your photo print upside down!

When you find that letter that you've been looking for, choose an angle that gets rid of distracting backgrounds as much as possible. A simple background will make your letter show better in the picture.

Then get as close as you can to the letter. For example, if you find a letter in a winter cornfield, crouch way down and get close enough so that the cornstalks that make the letter fill the viewfinder. (Don't try to get closer than three feet, though, because most cameras won't focus when you're that close.)

If you are ready to shoot, steady the camera first by resting your elbows on your knees, your hips, or on the ground. This will help you get sharp photos. Squeeze the shutter button down, without jerking the camera. Take lots of shots, from as many good angles as possible. Don't be disappointed if you only get one or two good shots from a roll of film. This is to be expected, even for experienced photographers.

When you finish your picture taking, write down where and when you took each photograph. You may want to have those notes later, when you put your alphabet collection together.

Photography equipment

Begin taking pictures with a point-and-shoot camera. If you really like photography, consider getting an SLR (single-lens-reflex) camera or a good digital camera and a tripod. The SLR camera lets you look directly through the lens, instead of looking through the viewfinder. If you have an SLR, you can buy different lenses for different kinds of photography. For example, a close-up lens will let you photograph things as close as a few inches away. A telephoto lens will bring faraway things closer.

A tripod is useful for holding your camera steady. This is especially important when there isn't lots of light. Your lens will need to be open longer then, and any jiggling will make the photo blurry. When you use a tripod, don't just shoot from eye level. Walk around your subject and choose the best angle for your shot. Hold your camera in position, set up the tripod so that it will hold the camera in that position, and then mount your camera on the tripod. It's a good idea to have someone else to help you with this tricky maneuver!

If you do buy an SLR camera and a tripod, remember that expensive equipment is not necessary to get great results. Careful, patient looking, along with creativity and good technique, are needed. You make the pictures; the camera, the lens, and the tripod do not.

Sketchbooks

If you don't want to use a camera, a sketchbook is a low-tech, wonderful way to collect letters. You won't have to worry about not having enough light for your film, jiggling the camera, or getting too close for the camera to focus.

Pack your sketchbook and some drawing supplies into a backpack. Be sure to take along something firm for a drawing board and something to sit on, in case the ground is damp. Be patient when you work. Try drawing with pencil, charcoal, crayon, ink, or any combination of these. Try using several different media for the same letter to see which captures the letter in the way that you like best. Remember that you are drawing both a natural item and a letter, so your drawing should look like both.

If your letter is in a raised form, like the veins of a leaf, the bark of a tree, or a pattern in rock, you can do a crayon rubbing directly from the object. For the most natural look, peel and use a crayon that is close in color to the thing that forms the letter. Use fairly thin paper and a light hand at first, then experiment with different types of paper and amounts of pressure until you get a result you like.

You might find it interesting to have an alphabet that includes letters in several different media, or you may want them all to be the same. Either way, be sure to write where and when you drew the sketch in the bottom corner. Sign your name and add the drawing to your alphabet collection.

Show off your collection.

Your carefully collected alphabet deserves a proper presentation. If your letters are photographs, you can mount them in an album. A nice way to do this is with sticky corners. You can also use a glue stick or double-stick tape. Choose a page size and paper type that allow you to write a few notes about the day and place you took the photo, the object that you photographed, and any other things you want to remember. You may also want to try your hand at writing a poem or a story about each letter on its page.

If you collect your letters as drawings, a nice way to display your artist's alphabet is to mount each drawing on an individual sheet of heavy textured paper. Choose big enough sheets so there is room for you to add notes, poems, and stories about each letter. Be sure to do front and back covers, using additional drawings mounted on lightweight cardboard. These covers can be fun to create and will add to the beauty of your book. Then hole-punch each sheet and the covers. Bind everything together with small rings, yarn, or leather shoestrings.

Frame Your Name.

Another exciting way to show off your letters is to put just the letters in your name into a frame or onto nice-looking cardboard. If your name has more than one of the same letter in it, like the name Anne, you can either use the same photo or drawing for both N's or you can find two different N's to add variety. You also might like to frame just the first letter of your first name or just your initials.

Even if you don't find all 26 letters in the alphabet, finding the letters in your own name and displaying your work in a frame can be creative, beautiful, and satisfying.

FOLLOWING THE RULES

Your alphabet hunt may take you to local, state, and national parks. Each park has its own rules about where you can hike. Parks also have rules about not disturbing the natural features of the park. These rules usually say that you shouldn't damage, change, or remove anything—rocks, plants, sticks, birds' nests, feathers, or any other natural material—from the park. The park should be left just the way you found it. Take nothing away but photos and drawings. Leave nothing behind but your footprints.

Never try to look at a bird's nest in the summer. Summer is nesting time, and if you disturb a nest while eggs or babies are in it, the parents may abandon the nest. Then the eggs or babies will die. Wait until winter to look for nests.

There are many plants and animals in the United States that are considered "threatened" or "endangered" because their populations have shrunk so much. It is especially important to avoid disturbing any threatened or endangered species. If you wonder which species are having trouble, a U.S. Fish and Wildlife Service Web site lists them: http:/endangered.fws.gov/wildlife.html#Species

A good alphabet hunter will always obey these rules. The great thing about an alphabet hunt is that you can take away all the photos and drawings of nature you want without breaking any rules. Good hunting!

CPSIA information can be obtained at www.ICGtesting.com
Printed in the USA
LVIW01n2129080415
433853LV00007B/19